Life After Lupus

Lupus Journey 2

Francine L. Houston

HATCHBACK Publishing
Genesee MI

Life After Lupus
© 2018 by Francine L. Houston

All Scripture quotations, unless otherwise indicated, are taken from the Amplified Bible, Copyright © 1954, 1958, 1962, 1964, 1965, 1987 by The Lockman Foundation. Used by permission.
Scripture taken from *The Message*. Copyright © 1993, 1994, 1995, 1996, 2000, 2001, 2002. Used by permission of NavPress Publishing Group.

Published by: HATCHBACK Publishing LLC
                    Genesee, Michigan 48437
                    Since 2005
The views, opinions and words expressed in this book are those of the author and does not necessarily reflect the position of HATCHBACK Publishing LLC or its owners.

ISBN 978-1-948708-10-4

Cover Design: Cineik Media

Printed in the United States
For Worldwide Distribution

Dedicated

to
Jesus Christ who is the Savior and Lord of my life

Acknowledgments

Jesus Christ, God, Holy Spirit
To my future husband I don't know who you are, I pray for you, to our future children we have together, to a blessed future together

Katie Brooks (my mother)
Jerry Houston (father)
Theresa Copeny Houston (stepmother)
Ramos Ball Sr. (honorary stepfather)
Tammy Houston (sister)
Tina Brooks (sister)
Ramos Ball Jr. (brother)
Demetrius Bibbs (April) (brother)
Kimberly Richard Starks (sister)
Tewania Blackwell (sister)
Nekicia Luckett (sister)
Montrail Lee (brother)
Nikki Lee(Ronald)(sister)
Donte Lee (brother)
Brandy Lee (brother)
Jeremy Lee (brother)
Kremmy Walker (sister)
Marcus Lee(Santigus)(brother)
My nephew Isaac Houston
Extended family and friends
Viney and John Brown(aunt and uncle)
Jay and Courtney Brown(cousins)
Gary and Nikki Brown(cousin)
Gracie Pendelton(aunt)
Ethel Harris(aunt)
David Brooks(uncle)
Joseph Brooks(Birdie)(uncle)
Jacobli and Marla Brooks (cousin)
Columbus and Rosie Brooks (aunt and uncle)
the late Walter Pendelton Sr. (uncle)
the late Cleveland Brooks(uncle)
the late Francis Jackson(aunt)

the late Authur (Bud) Brooks (uncle)
the late Latoya Atkins (sister)
Jaron Houston (cousin/twin)
Darren Houston (cousin/twin)
Trina Macon (cousin)
Linda Macon (aunt)
Miranda and Bo Manns (cousins)
Bennie and Ashara Manns (cousins)
Louise and Kenneth Mannie (friends)
Janine Parham (friend)
Tammi Amerson (sister in Christ)
Saved in Style and everyone connected to it (SIS)
Esosa and Shereena Osai (friends)
Takeesha and Montrail Carr (cousins/friends)
Zslanda Richardson(sister in Christ/friend)
Katurah Atkins (cousin)
Ivory Jeff Clinton (friend)
James Williams (friend)
People who prayed for me that I knew that was praying and
those I didn't know who prayed
Word of Faith
House of Glory
Full Gospel

Table of Contents

Foreword

Francine Houston has powerful spiritual insight that is invariably unique and profound. The faith principles in this book provide faith tools needed to heal people from various sicknesses globally. This book is an essential read.

 Dr. Apostle Joseph Johnson

House of Glory International Church

Introduction

Recap of the last chapter of Lupus Journey: 2009

This introduction is just to catch up a little before I start the sequel. I left off going on a cruise with my friends from church to the Bahamas. This was at the end of the year 2009 in December, when the cruise prices had good rates). That was the high note of the year. Coming back to Michigan afterwards and facing the snow was another story. It was odd walking around Bahamas, and Florida with Christmas trees but no snow. They even had the gifts underneath the tree.

While on the cruise, there were a lot of activities. I first had to find my room and the burrito bar. I was really hungry. The people who make the beds on the carnival cruise ship like to make animals or shapes out of the towels. So every day, we would see a new shape or animal made out of towels. We had to dress up a lot. There was always a captain ball or something. I had to bring several evening gowns.

While back at home, our house was finally livable, so we moved back in. It was so clean, they fixed the holes in the wall from the robbers, taking the pipes. Our house had a fire, was not livable and people came and took things from our home. So, the rest of the year, I looked for work and did graphics. I was happy Obama was the President, but I still have to do my part. I never thought I would get a job because the President was Black.

So that Christmas, I was really thankful. I had a roof over my head even though I had a bad fire and I was in it, I just went on my first cruise, and my health was excellent. Prior to the excellent report of health, I had bad seizures and a lupus flare-up. They put me back on medicine to balance me out and I got tested to see if I needed medicine. The tests came back good, so I was off the hook.

Chapter One

2010

In 2010, I was approaching the tender age of 30 in March that year, I wanted things to be better, but I was really rushing the process. I had several different jobs including tutoring high school children in Detroit, web designing at FFP Music, and I worked a few days at the graphic place on top of a liquor store. I decided to get into fashion by being an intern for the Vanity fashion show that year. I was really behind the scenes at that time, I was one of the dressers for the show. During this year, my lupus was actually in remission, no symptoms, no medicine. I was actually looking forward to vacation at the end of the year again. I became "addicted to cruises since 2009." I was obsessed with vacations. They really helped me to relax, help me not have any lupus flare-ups and just enjoy my life. My good friend since IADT College, Will invited me to cruises. In college I was in fashion and he was in web design.

Meanwhile being an intern in Vanity, I really saw how fashion was. I ended up being a graphic intern for a lady starting a magazine. She was also in the show as well but she spend more time doing her own thing and not helping with the show.

This experience in fashion showed me how we didn't really help one another. Everyone seemed to want the spotlight and not really working as a group. I was just an intern but one of my friends from college was trying to point me out as a designer (this happens years later). I stayed in the background I was not ready for this yet.

While going to the try-outs for Vanity, my cousin BJ and sister Tina wanted to be models for the show. I took them with me, as well as BJ's friend. The only one picked was her. My cousin BJ later became a personal trainer and fitness model though. While Tina did hair, she modeled for me later on. So, on the day of the show, I was helping dress the models and was asked to watch a camera. I made a mistake and put it down while helping other models. The camera was misplaced.

The lady that asked me to watch the camera was very upset and told me off. I was working back there with my friend Brandy who was a fashion stylist. She was one of the dressers as well. She helped me try to look for the camera but we couldn't find it. I tried to make it up to the lady by assisting to buying another camera but this didn't work because it was the memories that she couldn't bring back, she said. That is what made it valuable to her. I ended up crying at the end of the day like a baby. I was really stressed out because she was angry with me, the drama with the magazine lady and my decision to help with this show anyway.

I must have gained some trust or they were trying to figure me out. Ebony gave me another chance to work with her later on.

For the majority of 2010, I was changing jobs. I ended up getting a cleaning job for the summer. One of my friends told me God was preparing me for my husband. I guess so. I still do some forms of art though. I am an artist/designer. This is what I do. My sister Tammy and I still went to a lot of prayer meetings out in Detroit/Southfield.

I had a rider in my car from working for Labor Ready. She was only 18 to 19 years old. She lived with her mother who was bi-polar. My father is bi-polar but I never lived with him. She always had a lot of problems at home. I ended up talking to her about Jesus, church, and seeing if she had a relationship with Jesus.

I started doing more business as well. I meet a young lady later on that year who wanted to start a digital magazine.

God told me to join Faith groups. The training started in October that year, while still singing in the choir. I ended up having another person as my host, she became a coach, later on. I was her assistant for the group.

I really switched jobs a lot this year. I even applied on Craigslist. I ended up getting a scam job on Craigslist. They sent me a check for a huge amount of money and wanted me to give it to an orphanage. I thought it was real until I actually went to the bank to cash the check. The bank made me hold the check to make sure it cleared. The people were acting like I was taking too long to cash the check. It was good I did because the check was fake, and I would have owed the bank.

Even though I had a job as a housekeeper, my co-worker and I ended up getting hired full-time through the apartment complex and not the staffing agency. This was good news. However, I was saving and putting money aside for my vacation in December. My job honored the vacation and other time off I needed since it was before I was actually hired in.

At the end of the year, I went on my vacation in December on the Carnival Cruise Caribbean Cayman Islands, St. Thomas Virgin Islands and Cozumel, Mexico. I really needed the vacation. I went with a group of friends

from church.

Chapter Two

2011

It was the beginning of the year when my sister, Tina Brooks gave me a project to complete: her prom dress. I only had a few months though, plus working full-time job. I sewed Tina's prom dress, she graduated from high school this year. Despite working I still had a lot on my plate: Doing a website for someone, making the dress and doing a fashion show.

I was asked by my friend Brandy to be her lead stylist for her fashion show. It ended up with her doing a lot more directing, than I did. I felt like I was there trying to help them with the show. I was learning the ropes behind the scenes, working on struggles with my sisters. We did a photoshoot with my friend, another graduate from the College for Creative Studies.

I went to School of the Bible at the end of the year. At that time, I was working as a housekeeper at an apartment complex. I was still trying to get back into my field of computers. My Aunt Viney would get at me about it. My cousin Gary is a mechanical engineer and builds computers, so this type of stuff runs in the family.

I still had a rider in my car. She finally moved out of her mother's house and found an apartment to stay in. I was still in faith groups at that time so I would bring her with me to the house meetings. She really was going through a lot but both of us were at our job. Our management at Normandy Square was changing. The new management fired all of the staff except one and myself. They made us sub-contractors.

Chapter Three

2012

From January through September of this year, I was a graphic/web/marketing intern for ERollins group, I started FH designs styles in the city fashion show and a pre-gospel fest. I also went on a week cruise for 32nd birthday and completed my 2nd year and last year of School of Bible 2.

In December of last year, I applied for an internship at a fashion marketing company. I received a call in January of the next year. I became an intern for ERollins group.

My brother Montrail Lee was up here from Mississippi at this time. He had a very hard time in the military because of his mental condition from the war. My sister Tammy decided to become his guardian. That was when the trouble began. I know my sister and I have kind hearts like our mother, but sometimes we should pray first before helping anyone.

Her making this decision caused a lot of controversy in

the family. My own father really showed a side no one wanted to see. He was even against the guardianship and was thrown into jail because he harassed people in court, especially Tammy. He went toe to toe with every word she said to the judge, as if her helping her own brother was wrong. It didn't make any sense to me or Tammy. Now I really wished I would have listened to my mother about leaving my dad side of the family alone. I was in Bible College at that time and prayed with my teacher. I wanted my father out of jail. I know he was wrong, even my teacher from People's Bible College did. I know my sister wanted to do the right thing and I even helped.

The situation got so bad, my sister had to put a PPO on our father. She got someone from a church who was also a cop to accompany her. My father pulled out a rifle from his trunk. However, they still gave him the PPO.

This is when I decided to spend less time with that side of the family because it was too much drama. I wasn't getting killed over money. Everyone outside of our family wanted

Tammy to continue being the guardian of my brother Montrail. I was only the voice of reason. I didn't want anyone to get hurt.

For many years, there have been a feud with my dad's side, the Houston's and my mother's side, the Brooks. I didn't want to resurrect strife in my own family. If anyone else find out what my dad did, World War III would have broken lose.

There were a lot of challenges I faced along with my sister. Yet I knew I would overcome and I overcame.

The poem *I Will Overcome*   3/10/12

Despite it all, I will overcome.

From the looks of things, my life seems gloomy.

Broken dreams, harsh realities consume me.

My hope is Christ is the only thing that moves me.

My hopeless situation is an opportunity for God to step in and get the glory.

This will only make my testimony an even more glorious story.

When everything in life seems to be going wrong,
when my mind is consumed by sad, sappy songs,
I put my faith in God and know this battle is His all along.
I will overcome.

Despite everything I see, I know I have the victory.
The enemy constantly trying to pursue me with thoughts of
defeat and misery, but by reading your word and building
my faith, singing songs of victory and praying on my face,
I will overcome.
I will overcome by the blood of the lamb and the word of
my testimony, and not love
my life unto death.
I will overcome because you, Jesus, are with me.
You never leave me nor forsake me,
You're closer than a brother,

I love you more than my own mother.

I put you first in everything I do,

I put my plans aside and I pursue you.

Your will God and not my own.

Thank you, God for replacing those sobby songs.

Despite what I see,

You are with me along,

I will overcome.

Broken relationship, broken dreams, harsh family

situations, hopeless realities,

I will allow you God, to re-write my reality.

I will overcome.

Despite what I see,

God always gives His people the victory.

The worse the situation, the more we see God's glory.

I will overcome.

Despite it all,

God gives a measure of faith to us all.

So, despite what I see, God's word will never fail.

With God I will always prevail.

I will overcome.

Despite situations in life,

The battle is the Lord's and He is going to fight my battles.

God always wins.

In God's word, He shows up on time again and again,

since I'm his child, He will fight for me.

He will show up on my behalf and deliver me.

Despite the pain and misery I see,

I will overcome.

Lord you will always come through,

You give me instructions on what to do.

I look to you when I am going through,

So, I will always overcome.

I will overcome.

I overcame.

I went on a week long cruise during the time I was in
School of the Bible. I needed a break. It was around my 32
birthday.

Chapter Five

2013

This year consisted of completing FH designs, being a freelance graphic designer, social media/graphic intern, and graduating from School of the Bible 2. I also did various graphic work, dream 2 and 3, a rooftop fashion show, the Universal Shade fashion show and started a men's line. I sewed a prom tuxedo, church suits, wrote an article for "Lupus Now" magazine, applied for grad school U of Michigan-school of information, and became Art Director of Layby Advertising in December.

In the beginning of this year, January 2013, my sister and I worked at PC Treasures where we packed all the electronics for companies. One day we didn't carpool because I wasn't called into work and we worked through a staffing agency. So, she just worked there that day. Before she got on the highway, a car hit her and her car looked pretty bad. She called our cousin Gary, who we called

"Face", to come pick her up. He was leaving one job to go to another. The tow truck came and found her car and she had to take it to a mechanic.

I was still in Flint with my mom, younger siblings and my cousin BJ who had moved in. I found out about her car accident and went out there to help. My mother always thinks I was the rescue crew or something. I wasn't sure if it was a good move to be in Royal Oak for a minute. I had clients and was starting to pick up for FH, so I had to do something. It was a family emergency.

So, I drove out there out and realized my sister needed a caregiver. She could barely move her neck. She wanted to sue the man who hit her, but he didn't have car insurance. So, she decided to sue her insurance company AAA. I didn't know it would come back and bite the rest of the family. So, I stayed there for about four months or so to take her to work, since we worked at the same place. She had to go to physical therapy as well and she had another roommate for a while.

AAA actually took our family off the insurance a few months later. I still don't know why. We ended up switching to another car insurance company. I thought it happened because Tammy sued AAA over the car accident.

While Tammy was recovering from her car accident, I was in my last session of School of the Bible. I also was starting to have the beginnings of a lupus flare-up, a lupus relapse. I was experiencing symptoms off and on this year. I was going to several different doctors. During January of this year, I went to a new doctor and new hospital as well. She was a little off. I didn't like the way she treated me, so I went back to my old doctor and hospital. No matter what blood test I was taking, they thought they saw Lupus. In July, I had a clean slate of health however I had to go back in September. September came and the rheumatologist wanted me to take Plaquenil again. The same thing happened in November. This time I even brought the meds but didn't take them. I found a new doctor in Detroit who was a natural homeopathic/holistic doctor. She got me detoxing on spinach and water the first week that I went to see her. If God healed me before, I knew He could do it again. I believed I would be healed.

Tammy and I were finally seeing face to face about issues we had with each other and we were doing a four-month change, working on ourselves and our relationship as sisters.

I remembered what I learned years ago about Lupus. I learned to take care of myself. It seemed simple but little things like not getting enough sleep, not eating right, being around people that didn't treat me right, meant I had to keep learning to love myself. I know this is the first rule of love is to "love your neighbor as yourself." But if you don't love yourself how can you love your neighbor? So now I try my hardest to get enough sleep, eat healthy food, and surround myself with people who love me, plus get the spa treatment.

After the visit with my doctor, I realized I had to make a lot of changes. I had to eat healthier. For three years I was Lupus-free. I enjoyed my life, went on cruises, fashion shows, Bible College, and more. My doctor called and asked me a range of questions. My blood had a lot of inflammation. However, I was told it was reversible and I would be getting a new regime the upcoming week. I had to make more lifestyle changes.

I learned that there were toxins in my blood. It could be from the actual blood line from birth. My dad dealt with a lot of drugs and liquor. I just wanted to get to the root of the problem and actually solve it. I couldn't solve it but I prayed that God revealed something to my Christian doctor.

I just felt like I had been fighting this blood disease for a long time. When I thought it was over, I relaxed and tried to live life before lupus came in it. I had to stop that way of life and conform to a healthier, relaxed life instead of stressful life. I realized I took things too seriously. I had to let things roll off of me.

I went back to the blood results next Monday from my new doctor in Detroit, Michigan. She actually is my cousin-in law's best friend. I had to switch doctors because I was not about to take Plaquenil for the rest of my life. I learned my blood issue of lupus could be reversed. Thank God. I tried to take care of myself and look nice for myself.

During one week in this year, the cities of Mt. Morris, Flint, Grand Blanc, and even parts of Lansing experienced a blackout that lasted for a week or so. My stubborn family and I tried to stick it out for four days. During that time my Uncle came with a generator that kept us warm for the rest of the day and night. My other Uncle came by with blankets, presents, food and lights. By the next day which was Christmas it was too cold for us to bare. We ended up going to Tammy's condo and spending the rest our

Christmas over my Aunt's house, who was also our landlord. She was really upset with us when we didn't contact her when it first happened. We ended up staying with her for two days. I watched so many movies and we ate very well.

However, at the end of the year, our family dealt with the tragic death of Tina's oldest sister LaToya Atkins. She was only thirty-five years old. I remembered her from grade school up to high school. Later on, we saw her at the family restaurant, Southern Bell. She was getting into church and starting going. She was a year older than my sister Tammy. It was a sudden death, she was just having a headache. She went to Regional Hospital and told them she was not feeling well. They checked her, didn't see anything wrong with her and sent her home. She ended up having a blood clot in her brain and went into a coma. Tina stayed by her sister. She even didn't want to go to college anymore. I went to see her at the hospital and prayed for LaToya.

She didn't get out of it. We had her funeral in December of 2013. It was tragic, unexpected and fear started to grip me. I began to be afraid that I would die prematurely. I knew that sounded strange but it had happened it my family before. My cousin Cassandra died a few years prior, after a stomach surgery. The surgery went well but one day after seeing her son off to school, she died in her house.

Chapter Five

2014

During this year, I was a part of shades of u, Stylez 2014, I wrote for Lupus Now magazine in one of the issues, created an online store for FH Designs, saw May Dream 4 but did not participate and worked with art impact marketing.

My Lupus Journey book was finished but not published yet and Isaac was born May 14th, 2014. He came out trying to hold his own head up as a newborn. He was very advanced.

I thought I would be the art director but it was placed on hold. They were waiting for the creative brief from Target and Brauman, so I was getting ready for this fashion show and book to come out. My sister was here from Hong Kong and moving back to the states to Massachusetts. I also had the GRE test, was working eight hours and still had to handle social media demands. I had not heard from my mentor yet, so I had to play catch up. I prayed that this fashion show went well because I was also starting my guy's line.

The Flint water crisis happened around April of 2014, when Flint's water was contaminated. My sister Tina did hair and her clients were losing their hair, including me. I thought it was lupus, however it was more to it than that. People couldn't take showers without breaking out. Lead was found in the water. My sister Tammy and nephew Isaac lived in Flint at that time as well. Tammy even went on television at a church she was volunteering for, to talk about the Flint water crisis. She mentioned my name and talked about how it affected my hands.

I must go forward.

I cannot look behind me.

I learned from my past mistakes.

But a new journey, new beginning is what I want to embrace.

So, I must move forward and not dwell on my past.

God wants to take me to new places, meet new people,

to dream again.

I cannot dwell on my broken heart from past relationships.

I must go forward so I can heal and live again.

(11-19-14)

Vehicle Fashion Week: November 12-15th

I was doing ok health wise back then. I was trying to go

vegan back then. I talked to another natural homeopathic

doctor. She told me to go vegan to clean my skin up. I

assumed being vegan would help my blood too.

During this year, I had a typical day just going to the

dentist to get my teeth cleaned. The cleaning went well, I

didn't bleed as much or have any cavities. However, a few

days after work my gums were bleeding. I worked at nights

for Birch Run area schools so I had to make an

appointment in the morning. I went to the dentist and they

told me I had an abscess and had to take antibiotics. They

38

were working for a while. But after a week, my face started looking swollen. I would pray and before I went to work, it would be normal. I made another appointment with my dentist. My abscess left, and I got off the medication. However, the swelling continued. I didn't know it was the beginning stages of kidney failure, lupus nephritis.

Universal Shade: December 28, 2014

Today I woke up with a rash on my face and tried to call or text a friend that I couldn't be in the show. She suggested that my sister Tina went instead. Tina said no. I went to church and felt better, so I went to the fashion show as well. The swelling went down and my face cleared up enough to do the fashion show. I got someone to put make-up on me so you couldn't tell that I wasn't looking like myself. I found some models to wear my clothes. I had some really close friends in the front at the vendor table. I was nervous because I gained weight and couldn't wear my size 5. I had to wear Tina's jeans which was a size 7. I didn't know how I gained the weight. I didn't know this was the beginning stages of kidney failure. I still went out there and they played "Walking" by Mary Mary. They took pictures at the end of the runway and I smiled as usual with my model.

When the pictures came out however my older sister had a problem of my picture. She kept on saying "You don't look right." I told her I wasn't feeling good. She gave me the third degree, literally. I didn't feel like arguing with her.

I kept having bad dreams. I had a dream that I was dead in a coffin. Everyone was at my funeral. I had another dream that I was in my car with the engine on. My hands were tied up and foot on the aerator. I was on Cypress drive right in front of my Aunt Ethel's house. It seemed so real. My mother was there saying, "Bye Francine." Maybe she didn't see I was tied up and couldn't use my arms. I woke up in a cold sweat. I kept on telling myself, "I will live and not die and proclaim the works of the Lord."

Chapter Six

2015

I received the *Pray Like a Wife* book.

Luke 8:43-48 King James Version (KJV)

43 And a woman having an issue of blood twelve years, which had spent all her living upon physicians, neither could be healed of any,

44 Came behind him, and touched the border of his garment: and immediately her issue of blood stanched.

45 And Jesus said, Who touched me? When all denied, Peter and they that were with him said, Master, the multitude throng thee and press thee, and sayest thou, Who touched me?

46 And Jesus said, Somebody hath touched me: for I perceive that virtue is gone out of me.

47 And when the woman saw that she was not hid, she
came trembling, and falling down before him, she declared
unto him before all the people for what cause she had
touched him, and how she was healed immediately.
48 And he said unto her, Daughter, be of good comfort: thy
faith hath made thee whole; go in peace.

Fight for My Life

Like a thief in the night you come and steal from me,
drain me of my energy, distort the best parts of me.
When the thief became like a wolf growling and tearing
away, Lupus tries to make a home within but the Holy
Spirit dwells therein.
The struggle is real; the fight to believe that what I see is
temporary verses permanent.
The mirror became my friend instead of a nightmare; my
words I speak become healing instead of a curse.

My life is extended and not shortened.

My surroundings are not depressing but a delight

I must stay engaged in this fight; the fight for my life.

1/17/15

Trying to fit in a mold not created for me,

trying to be someone I am not called to be.

I can only be me.

I am free to be me, to transform into the person God called

me to be,

to except myself as I am,

to love myself despite of my flaws,

to see myself as God sees me,

to love myself unconditionally.

I must be free to be me.

  January 19, 2015 was my last day of work as a custodian

at Birch Run Area Schools. For weeks I would come in

swollen and in pain. My co-workers would either do my

job or help. They kept on telling the boss that I was sick. I really needed to take a day off. My boss really didn't care. There were several people that quit the job, so that meant extra buildings to clean. My boss kept on saying, "Once we hire more people, I will let you take a day off". It seemed like the Lord works in mysterious ways. The next day, I received a call early in the morning from my doctor at the time. She told me to go to the hospital and take a bed. I asked, "What?". She explained that my tests from the lab were not that good and that I needed to take the day off work. I had to work that afternoon, so I was really trying to go in. My family saw how much fluid I was retaining from low kidney function and begged me to stay home. I am a workaholic at times but this time I decided to take their advice. So, I called my job saying my doctor wants me in the hospital tomorrow because I am very sick. She still wanted me to come in that day. I called my doctor to see if I should to work that day and she agreed with my family about staying home. My boss was in her early 20's and she was going to write me up. I was more scared about that then my health, I needed to snap back into reality. I went over her head and called her boss. I told him the whole scenario and he said he would take care of it.

So I stay home and made an appointment for the next day to a kidney specialist in Grand Blanc. I had to get Tina to take me along with her friend Chelsea. I had to see the kidney specialist before I was admitted into the hospital. I was not there for too long. I went in the office and signed my name on the waiting list. The nurse called my name and I went back immediately. I had to do a urine test. I barely could go. I gave the cup back to the doctor and was told to go to McLaren. My Uncle John Brown and Aunt Viney had to drive me to the hospital. Tina and Chelsea had to go to work at the salon.

On departure to the hospital, it was a bad winter storm. I felt very heavy walking to their truck. They drove through the storm to the hospital. I had to go through emergency. I ended up waiting in the emergency area until they called my name. My Aunt Viney was there too. Once inside they weighed me and I had to get two blood transfusions. My blood was very low. I was so cold. I had to lay down in a bed inside of a room in the hospital. They gave me my IV there. The nurse came in with a big bag of blood and I had to sign off for it. The blood had to match my blood which is B-positive. The nurse gives me my first blood transfusion. I feel warmer but still need more blankets. My blood count went up, but not high enough so they give me another blood transfusion. I feel better but know I have more tests to go.

I had a kidney biopsy and two surgeries for dialysis. Dialysis became a part of my daily routine, three days a week at a dialysis center up the street from me. Lupus has taken its toll on my body again and almost caused total kidney failure. A renal diet was introduced to me while in the hospital. It became a part of my path to wellness.

Although I had two surgeries in the hospital, the kidney doctor wanted the catheter out of my neck and a fistula in my arm for dialysis. The fistula in my left arm was permanent and it made that arm weaker. I could not do as much as I would like. The word "disability" was roaming around the doctor's office. I had already given up my custodian job and was told not to "overwork" myself. I could not do physical labor jobs. So, I thought I was retired by the age of 34. I wanted to know my options.

I got back from the hospital on January 26th. I had to do a chemo treatment before I left. I was scheduled to take these IV injections every two weeks. They were for my kidney which was at stage 5 and needed a kidney transplant. When I went home, the doctor changed the chemo treatment to pills and I needed a caregiver. My cousins Jaron and Darren Houston came by and my mother didn't trip. It was a miracle. I had other visitors as well.

My cousin Darren volunteered to help but he had some issues going on. I guess you can't pick your help. Tammy came by and help when she could. I couldn't drive until my Prednisone dose was down to 20mg. So, most of the time

Tina had my car while I was at the hospital and Tammy had it when I got out of the hospital. I was at 80mg at the hospital. I felt very high. Every few weeks, I would taper down off the medicine. I had a mental struggle from this medication. It made me very moody and emotional, more than usual.

One day, my mom decided to be my caregiver. I was going to pay the person anyway. I was working with the state of Michigan to work out a wage for my caregiver. Darren still wanted to help and called to check up on me. He knew a lot about the renal diet, dialysis and the catheter.

The weirdest thing out of this is I had a new Facebook friend. He was older than me and found out I was sick, so he would send me scriptures and music. He was truck driver at the time so he would check on me while he was driving. I really didn't think much about it because when he got back to Michigan, I would never see him. I found out he had five children and a lot of baby mamas. He was a good friend during this traumatic time in my life.

My life changed, I faced the possibility of total disability, I was looking for student loan forgiveness for federal and some private loans. I had to shut down for two weeks and couldn't do physical labor. I had to go to McLaren hospital for a week and my whole life changed.

Good news was Tina was working on her salon and had enough rooms for other businesses. I decided to see about having a room there. I couldn't work from home anymore. I had bad "workaholic" issues already. I had to keep myself busy. Once I was better, I would run my businesses but not put a lot of pressure on myself.

When you are going through something, this is when you find out who your friends really are.

Found By the Love of Christ   2/1/15

Felt like I lost my identity, forgot who God called me to be. Labeled myself based off titles of this world, felt like a lost little girl.

50

But you called me a daughter of royalty.

Surrounded myself with the wrong influence

that tore me down and built me up.

Need real love not false counterfeit love that the world

offers.

Tired of getting manipulated by the enemy's schemes,

even friends and family seemed to become mean,

but I'm not a lost little girl but a woman, a daughter of

royalty.

2/10/15

Progression. Journal writing.

I feel like I have made progress today. With the help of my

sister, Tina and Jesus, especially I realized what I need to

change.

Lord, I need a filter.

Like a kidney filters toxins in the body,

to not be so mean to people that I think want to hurt me.

I am not an experiment. I have to look at myself as God's gift.

No more saying whatever comes to my mind, no more letting all my emotions ran away from me.

I have a choice. I choice to love me.

  People with lupus deal with these issues. I was dealing with it now. I was so concerned about people in general that I was focusing on what is most important. I really needed to count my blessings. Things were getting better. I have three months to make that change. I felt like a vegetable at times. I may have felt like I lost my mind but I gained Christ's mind.

  I began to count the things I was thankful for. I had a place to stay, food to eat, clothes on my back, my mother was still alive, my dad was still here and my brothers and sisters were alive.

Lord I thankful for everything you done for me.

I'm so grateful that you set me free.

I am walking in divine life,

wholeness, wellness, newness of life.

I must see myself the way God does. My sister told me she looked up to me. I never knew she looked at herself as a sidekick, working with me as for the fashion shows. I saw us as individual hard-working women. God told me I was free. My name meant free. I just needed to walk in it. It sounded so simple I just needed to do it but also get that filter for real. I didn't realize that I was being mean. When I was being mean to the doctor, I heard God say, "That's because you don't like doctors". I felt like I was acting like a "teenage Christian". I may have looked like a 16-year-old but I am 34 and need to "woman-up." Lord, help me.

I really worried about what people said. Dealing with lupus is a lot. I feel like I would either be considered as an experiment or a miracle. God told me I was His gift. I was so focused on making money and buying people's birthday presents, that I didn't see myself as a gift. I was so concerned about what I could offer people. I finally saw my worth. I wrote a poem called "Woman's Worth." I am not angel but human beings with needs. I learned to crucify my flesh though. Every month, during my period I have those urges but have kept them under control, practicing temperance and focusing on the fruit of self-control.

Right now, my focused is to love myself. A Minister texted me Mark 12:31:

"And the second is like, namely this, Thou salt love thy neighbor as thyself. There is none other commandment greater than these."

So, I took her advice. The enemy had been making me feel guilty about incest that happened years ago. It ran in our family but I know it will not go past my generation. I prayed that the cycle would end. I experienced incest with a male cousin years ago. I was instructed by God years ago to write a poem about it. I read it to an audience on my 26th birthday. I had a guilty conscious, even for other things I repented for and was forgiven for.

There is nothing new under the sun. Even in life, things seem to go in full circle or similar to the way that things happened in the past.

My experiences seemed so similar to the bible.

2 Samuel 13King James Version (KJV)

13 And it came to pass after this, that Absalom the son of David had a fair sister, whose name was Tamar; and Amnon the son of David loved her.

2 And Amnon was so vexed, that he fell sick for his sister Tamar; for she was a virgin; and Amnon thought it hard for him to do anything to her.

3 But Amnon had a friend, whose name was Jonadab, the son of Shimeah David's brother: and Jonadab was a very subtil man.

4 And he said unto him, Why art thou, being the king's son, lean from day to day? wilt thou not tell me? And Amnon said unto him, I love Tamar, my brother Absalom's sister.

5 And Jonadab said unto him, Lay thee down on thy bed, and make thyself sick: and when thy father cometh to see thee, say unto him, I pray thee, let my sister Tamar come, and give me meat, and dress the meat in my sight, that I may see it, and eat it at her hand.

6 So Amnon lay down, and made himself sick: and when the king was come to see him, Amnon said unto the king, I pray thee, let Tamar my sister come, and make me a couple of cakes in my sight, that I may eat at her hand.

7 Then David sent home to Tamar, saying, Go now to thy brother Amnon's house, and dress him meat.

8 So Tamar went to her brother Amnon's house; and he was laid down. And she took flour, and kneaded it, and made cakes in his sight, and did bake the cakes.

9 And she took a pan, and poured them out before him; but he refused to eat. And Amnon said, Have out all men from me. And they went out every man from him.

10 And Amnon said unto Tamar, Bring the meat into the chamber, that I may eat of thine hand. And Tamar took the cakes which she had made, and brought them into the chamber to Amnon her brother.

11 And when she had brought them unto him to eat, he took hold of her, and said unto her, Come lie with me, my sister.

12 And she answered him, Nay, my brother, do not force me; for no such thing ought to be done in Israel: do not thou this folly.

13 And I, whither shall I cause my shame to go? and as for thee, thou shalt be as one of the fools in Israel. Now therefore, I pray thee, speak unto the king; for he will not withhold me from thee.

14 Howbeit he would not hearken unto her voice: but, being stronger than she, forced her, and lay with her.

15 Then Amnon hated her exceedingly; so that the hatred wherewith he hated her was greater than the love wherewith he had loved her. And Amnon said unto her, Arise, be gone.

16 And she said unto him, There is no cause: this evil in sending me away is greater than the other that thou didst unto me. But he would not hearken unto her.

17 Then he called his servant that ministered unto him, and said, Put now this woman out from me, and bolt the door after her.

18 And she had a garment of divers colours upon her: for with such robes were the king's daughters that were virgins appareled. Then his servant brought her out, and bolted the door after her.

19 And Tamar put ashes on her head, and rent her garment of divers colours that was on her, and laid her hand on her head, and went on crying.

20 And Absalom her brother said unto her, Hath Amnon thy brother been with thee? but hold now thy peace, my

sister: he is thy brother; regard not this thing. So Tamar remained desolate in her brother Absalom's house.
21 But when king David heard of all these things, he was very wroth.

Incest

I wouldn't think it would happen to me; I buried this shame for no one to see. Everyone would think that your family would have your back, but they were the ones trying to get you behind your back. Waiting till you're asleep to take something precious away from you. Waking up to see you've been invaded by someone so dear to you. Wishing that maybe it's something I did to cause this attraction, and even feeling ashamed that you like this interaction. I watched this on television and I thought this wouldn't happen to me but God brought it back to my remembrance and I knew it had to be me as well. Burying hurt deep down for years will always resurface.

I'm happy when it did that.

God's mercy healing me and allowing me to share this with others, so I could be free, exposing the truth will only allow you to be free.

So, I'm sharing part of myself to warn others sometimes you may have to be cautious around your father, brother or even cousin. Sometimes this affection my go the wrong way. God can only fix this situation and help the person learn to look at you the right way.

As I was reading *Unshakable* by John Eckhardt, I found out autoimmune diseases are rooted in rejection. One of the causes of rejection is subjection to sexual molestation or incest. Other causes that related to me in my early life and later on, were constant criticism from parents, siblings, or authority figures, unhappy parents and grandparents who argue, fight, won't talk to each other, or only speak to their children. Their children will feel guilty and responsible. More possible causes for autoimmune diseases are alcoholism in one or both parents and destruction of the family home by fire or some natural disaster. Others include a family member convicting of a serious crime, parents showing no active interest in the progress of their children's schoolwork, sports activities, or leisure time pursuits.

Later in life comes rejection in love or a broken engagement, being fired from a place of unemployment for incompetency or being unable to find employment over a long period of time.

Rejection leads to self-hate and can often enter at an early age, even in the womb. When my mother was pregnant with me, my father shot at her as she was running across a field. This could have become a wound, and if left untreated become an infection. When a knitted sweater starts to unravel, it slowly comes apart. I also learned fear is a stronghold. From my sister Tammy sending me devotionals, I found out the opposite of fear is faith.

So while at the hospital, I had a lot to think about. I had many visitors, family and friends. I also remember it starts in the spirit realm before it manifests in the physical realm.

2/3/15

Lord this has been a journey. I don't where to begin. I had a very out of body experience. I didn't know if it was the drugs but it very supernatural. I wish I could have written as I was going through it. The blood of Jesus saved my life. I wore myself out. I could not go to siren with my mind racing. I felt like mind snatchers was coming for me representing the enemy. They looked like silver dart barter guys. I was locked up inside of car. I heard the Christians praying and fighting for my soul, but my mind, was slowing leaving my body. I could not function properly. It was as if my mind was a computer and it was breaking down. It was dying on me. The enemies almost took full control. I didn't know who I was. I was having an identity crisis. He kept asking me who I was, missing with my gender, the spirit of perversion was trying to take over me but I keep on fighting with the word of God. It happened more than yesterday. The enemy was really trying to wear me out. I kept repeating myself over and over again, really babbling. I felt totally out of control. The enemy was on my back. I realized in order to go to bed I had to pray a bedtime prayer. I prayed a sleep time prayer and then I saw a bright light in my room. My guardian angel was there and then I heard the gates of hell lock him up. It was like I was there in two dimensions.

The enemy was trying to convince me to be a part of his army. I belong to Christ. I am not about self-worship. I notice when working with non-Christian artists they worship themselves, and think they are gods. They have it all wrong. God made us like Him, but we worship God and not ourselves. It took me a minute to recognize this attack, but I had several attacks all at the same time. This "I stuff and self- help can get you in trouble. I say I am God's artist and in Christ. The enemy start with the "I" thing.

After I started getting sleep, it was so sound. I put on healing scriptures on and slept like a baby. I could feel God healing me.

Awaken Me Jesus

Like sleeping beauty, I was in sleep, God awakened my heart.

I felt dead inside with the issues of life weighting me down

God woo my heart and turned it upside down,

I don't know if I ever find love like this again,

it's so unconditional. I love God more than anything,

not based on emotions or feelings.

A deep knowing that He is with me, whatever I go through.

He 'll never leave me nor forsake me. His love is true.

Maybe I lost my first love in God. Maybe it was the fire I lost inside, but God rekindled it inside me. My first love

64

turned me away from the things I was doing for God, but God wanted me to just have Him alone. I really began to understand all I need is Him. God is my source. He is supplying all my needs. I really had to trust Him more in every area of my life. I was wearing my birthstone ring as a promise ring to stand on the promises of God. But it was just showing what was inside of me.

Based on Romans Chapter 8, nothing can separate me from love of God.

I ended up taking a cooking class with my sister Tammy, my mother, and my Aunt Gracie.

Cooking class assignment ideas to help with the renal diet:

Chicken Pot Pie (tailored to the renal diet)

Pasta, beans and greens

Salmon, green beans,

Chicken salad

Turkey burgers

Chicken with greens and a fruit

Chicken casserole

Pasta, garlic and butter

 I decided to write myself free and eat a snack. Those

steroids made me hungry.

 Good night.

4/13/15

Distractions come my way in different forms.

My mind set on impossible goals of the reaching goals on

my own.

Then it hit me what is my life worth to me?

Am I trying to impress everyone or try to speed up my

dreams?

After almost losing my life again, I know it God is taking

care of me.

Focus on what's important; my life, my health, my well-

being.

My focus is to obey Him and what He wants me to do,

not get caught up or focus so much on my cash flow but my blood flow.

My bank account verses my blood count; I realize I have to be alive to see the blessings of God, so I am focusing on my healing and not so much business because my health goes before it.

My life is important to me.

My health is important to me.

I took it lightly for too long.

When I wrote this poem, I was still on dialysis and was trying to hurry up and get off it. My mind was on the next fashion show or something. My mind was so far off in fame, fortune, movies, lights, camera, and action. I had to come down from cloud nine. I was used to going and coming as I pleased.

5/10/15

After I got prayed for, it seemed like I got attacked. I was already going through enough with Lupus. I almost died this year. I didn't take my life lightly anymore. I was not going to let anything or anyone get me down. It was Mother's Day today and all I could give my mom was a card. I was not working like I'd used too. I was forced to give up my job. I was going to Aldan with Tammi Amerson on Tuesday to see where the place was at. I would have liked to work there because it was for the disabled people. With my left arm having a fistula in it, I would be considered disabled. The doctors did not plan on reversing it either.

The next week would be an easy week but I planned to be gone if I could. No arguments for me. I was not even looking forward to July 4th. I needed a house or an apartment or something. I didn't like the way I was treated here at times. I considered moving when I could.

The next couple of months would be trying for me. I had to find a way to keep my head up. I got prayer for my finances so I had to trust God. I didn't want to overreact because it would raise my blood pressure and I didn't want to get sick again. I didn't vent on Facebook but I wrote how I felt.

With the experience of incest, I always wanted my innocence back.

6/14/17

Innocence

In a world where innocence is not the norm,

the world wants us to conform

to be like them in everything we do

but I must transform and follow you, God.

3/24 2015

What was I becoming? I needed a quiet meek spirit but I felt like I had to be ratchet for others to stop treating me bad. Lord help me stay in love. I represent You right. You even had to say certain things as well. Give me the words to say. I turned 35 today. Help me see myself as that. I was in transition. I'd just found out high blood pressure lead to strokes. I did not know this. My health was a priority to me. I had to take it seriously. I knew everything would work out for me. My mother would not take my car away from me or I would be broke and living in poverty or sick. God told me that He got me. I really was thankful to see 35. Thank you God, for living to see this age.

4/30/2015

I was down to one day of dialysis. However this day I took a test to see if I need dialysis anymore. It only lasted about an hour. I met the "legendary Reggie" who left dialysis to go to Atlanta. When he went to Atlanta, he tried to set up dialysis there. They told me when I went on my Chicago trip in March not to pull a "Reggie". I tried to tell him if he stuck to the diet, he would do better. He was not listening to me. I told him I would pray for him. He told me how to get rid of cramps by stripping down to just his t-shirt and underwear. It was cool up at the RRC. I didn't know about that. I thought Reggie was cute, but he was not saved. So that thought left after he opened his mouth.

I was a bit excited. I really wanted to find out if I needed dialysis anymore. I figured I would find out the next day, May 1st when the Avengers movie came out.

Looking back from January of this year, I went through a lot in a short amount of time. I had to quit my job at GRBS as a custodian, get on dialysis in McLaren, two blood transfusions, about four surgeries related to dialysis, dealing with SSI and DHS. That day I took a test today to see if I needed dialysis anymore. I was grateful to be alive

71

and be totally healed and set free. I was still looking

forward to school in July for eight weeks. I ended up

working instead.

  I got my mom her Mother's Day card. I found a dress form

for cheap on Jo-Ann's website for an order I had. I had to

watch my budget.

5/17/15

Today I testified at my old church. It was different there

now. It may not be like the word of faith, but I liked it

there. I was at stage three of the kidney disease with lupus,

which meant if I stuck to the renal diet, I would not be on

dialysis nor need a kidney transplant. So, I told my

testimony for the Glory of God.

  I don't just want healing, I want to be whole. No more

debt, poverty or sickness. Like the lady with the issue of

blood was healed and made whole. I wanted to be healed

and made whole. Nothing missing or broken in my life. I

wanted things to better than they were before I ever got

sick. I had to believe this was the year where I would be

healed, the year where a lot of my debts would be taken care of, the year I wanted to meet my future husband. I got so tired of being prophesied over but not meeting anyone. I was finally praying for the brother though. I believed it. I actually started praying again that I would meet him. Besides, I heard God say he was coming.

The year I actually had a job that I enjoyed and would not try to kill me. I was like any other person, I wanted to be happy. I didn't want to stay home the other day but it came down to my health versus hair. I would choose health any day. The catheter in my neck was coming out soon. I was nervous. The fistula would stay permanently. I thanked God for favor and inspiration. From my experiences in this year, I got the concept of loving myself despite of how selfish people think I am. When I really started loving myself, I did not allow others to mistreat me.

I was looking forward to gardening this year. I was sticking to eating right for me and making sure I was alive. I thanked God for healing me. I was told I would not see stage three and would need a kidney transplant. I prayed that I would not need one but my kidney remained healthy.

I trust God despite of what I see.

I know with Him I always have the victory.

When obstacles come my way, I don't know what to do

God shows me a way out,

so I should never doubt.

This month was rough especially not working. I had an interview next week. If I started I may have had to charge gas money just to get there unless they started me in June. I didn't even know when my next surgery is. I hoped it was Monday. I just wanted to get it out of the way.

5/31/15

Tammy was ministering to someone who was about to be homeless and was considering suicide. I remembered writing a short story about a woman thinking about committing suicide and what might have been going on in her mind, like the devil voice versus the Lord. It could be a mental battle but at the end of my story, she decided to live. I just prayed in reality he decided to live, nothing is worth losing your life for. I remembered some of my family facing homelessness and even me in 2009 when our house caught on fire. We all had to stay strong and I was grateful for my Aunt Ethel for letting our family stay with her. It took the rest of that year to get our house back up and going.

I just hoped he listened to the right voice and stayed around this earth. Maybe he would decide to be a Christian. As Christians we should show the love of Christ by the way we live. This had been a very trying year for Tammy and myself in different circumstances. I know I had to use my faith for just about everything especially when I was not working and did not get aid yet. This month of June, I did not look at it as a hardship but a comeback. Hey, if Janet

Jackson could come back for a world tour, I could come

back, with the Lord's help, of course.

7/5/15

You're too big

You're too small.

You're too fat.

You're too skinny.

You're too dark.

You're too light.

You're not like him.

You're not like her

You're too educated.

You don't have enough education.

You're overqualified.

You're under qualified.

The standards of this world will keep you unqualified to be you. To not be good enough for their standards of life. Glad I don't live for their approval but seek God's standards and approval for my life.

8/31/15

It was the end of prayer boot camp. I was hearing from God so clearly now because of prayer boot camp. Today was our graduation day. I didn't go see Jan because I needed some sleep and since I was closer to God, I didn't feel that she was needed now.

Yesterday there were a lot of people's birthdays or anniversaries: My Aunt's birthday and would have been anniversary but she was widowed. It was also Latoya Atkins birthday yesterday. Tina went to her grave too. I said a prayer for Aunt, Tina and the whole family. Death is hard to swallow sometimes. It took me years to get over my grandma's death. It felt like I lost a mother, then Uncle

Bud and Aunt Francis. But that was enough thinking about the dead.

I had to stay happy. I couldn't let this get to me. I had a near death experience during this year that I didn't plan to relive. I am even giving up overtime before I am even asked. My stomach was so messed up because of the food I ate and my time of month, I was just trying to get through the day.

My sister went to visit our father. I guess he had forgiven her. They were beefed out for years over Montrail's guardianship. If we had to do it over again I wished she didn't take guardianship of Montrail. It was too much. Even Carolyn my cousin was right about staying out of it. I didn't talk to her that much anymore. I tried to do business with her but that didn't work out either.

Think positive thoughts. Think happy thoughts. There was a picnic on Thursday at work and I was looking forward to it. There was also a lupus walk coming up and I was seeing about my book being published.

December 8th 2015 - Day 38 of the Prayer Challenge

At the beginning of this challenge I felt a bit defeated and in a losing battle in a lot areas in my life. I let people use me, sacrificed time and energy, and I was not taking proper care of myself. I had to let people go, it hurt but what hurt most was the damage it did to my health. I am still recovering from the lupus flare up since January of this year. There were tremendous benefits of this prayer challenge though outwardly and inwardly. Learning a new step at work, getting meds lowered at my next kidney doctor visit, receiving an excellence award in fashion and winning two free plane tickets.

However, I was praying about the green light competition for business. I was not prepared. Just like I was not ready to go back and serve in church. I need you God to heal me from lupus and lupus related things. I can't go far without my health. Some acquaintances didn't see that but I do. I was in a tangled situation with Naomi which I was trying to get out of. I had no choice but to stay away because my health was important to me. I stressed this to her but it went in one ear and out the other. So instead of saying I was just doing it. I didn't want to end up like my Aunt who helped people so much but neglected herself. I planned on living to see years to come. This lupus situation I was in is pretty serious so I couldn't take it lightly. I was improving but God was telling me to slow down and get rest. I couldn't get up and go as much as I used to or it would take a toll on my immune system. I went to the primary doctor today for test results. I was praying for good news. I may have seemed selfish for not helping Naomi but God said stay out of it. Naomi was getting a divorce from her husband. I was praying that they stayed together. I was not trying to be in the middle of it.

Chapter Seven

2016

1/25/16

I have a drive, ambition, in spirit I am free-flowing

But physically I felt challenged at times. I forgot or tried to

forget what happened the day I became a liability to many.

I tried to forget it and not remember it, not remember I was

considered disabled.

I wanted to try to rise above it but everything reminded

me of it. I tried to leave and run and hide from it but I was

stuck with it. It was a part of me now. I was still saddened

at times that I couldn't pursue my dreams because of this

liability, this disability hindered me.

I forgot about the thorn in my flesh that I couldn't take

out, it was depressing at times but if this was the year of

filling in the blank, then I needed faith for debt freedom

especially the federal and private ones. I felt like I was

fighting a never-ending battle. Would I ever win? Would I

receive the things I have been believing for so long? Would I persevere until it actually came?

Genesis 12:1

[1] The LORD had said to Abram, "Leave your native country, your relatives, and your father's family, and go to the land that I will show you.

[2] I will make you into a great nation. I will bless you and make you famous, and you will be a blessing to others.

[3] I will bless those who bless you and curse those who treat you with contempt. All the families on earth will be blessed through you."

I was still at Aldan, I had finally published Lupus Journey part 1, I had my businesses Cineik Media and F.H. Designs, still did fashion shows, and had moved to Lansing to be close to Aldam144.

Shortly after moving, I was in the component department in the apparel manufacturing. I was doing a certain step that required my hands to stretch out. I ended up having to wear

a brace on my wrist, take prednisone for a few weeks and

go to physical therapy. The swelling went down but I was

in a lot of pain. I was instructed to look for a different job

or else I had to wear a brace and go through this process.

So I started the process of looking for another job,

meanwhile I was moved back to barteching but was still in

apparel manufacturing.

5/2/16

I am not hopeless,

not a woman in distress

not fearful or what may happen next.

I know God has me in his hand,

He has the master plan.

Despite what the doctors may think,

the reports may show,

my doubts disappear,

my faith continues to grow.

The images of death try to flood my mind,

but God's grace steps in to remind

me that without the body, I am one with Christ.

The Lord gave 120 years

so, I have no fears.

The symptoms may come and go,

but I believe I will wake up tomorrow.

Death where is your sting?

Jesus took it and gave me the victory.

5/2/2016

Change

Can my life have a happy ending?

Can I forget the past and have a new beginning?

Can I get rid of my old thinking that things will never

change?

Thinking that it will always remain the same,

can I imagine having my own place, enough space?

A place I can call my own; can break free from sickness

that has been dragging me down for years when I think it's

gone it reappears.

Can I expect change?

Can I imagine God answering all of my prayers even the

ones I haven't even spoken on?

Can I expect change?

Can I expect the next guy I met be the one and not run

away when times get rough?

Can I expect change?

I better expect change,

only when I believe things will change they will,

everything doesn't have to remain the same.

With God all things are possible, so I believe the things I

am believing for will come to pass.

Now, not later not in the future.

Faith is now so I better expect change.

My suddenly has come and

my life will never be the same.

I moved to Lansing June 1st of 2016. I waited so long

because I needed to save up money for the move. I had to

buy things for the apartment. I was approved in March but

still needed to save for the security deposit. My job

happened to give me the money for the deposit. So, when I

got out to Lansing, I went to Runway Lansing to get my

business going out here. They immediately put me in a

retail class that interfered with my work schedule. I tried to

work around it anyway.

The first Saturday of the move to Lansing, I went to the

writer's meeting. Everyone either had their book getting

printed or published. I just sat there like a deer with the

headlights on. The facilitator came up to me and asked me was I ready to be published? At this point, I was not in business with my business partner and wanted to self-publish. I didn't know anything about that process. I ended up using a publishing company for my first book, *Lupus Journey*.

6/4/16

Survival of the fittest.

I push, I sacrifice, I dream.

I give all the things I think I don't need.

My focus was on survival,

not trying to keep up with the Joneses,

not trying to impress,

but I got tired of living check to check.

I felt like I was just surviving in life,

not thriving to be my best.

Focus on the now and not the future,

now I thrive to please God,

give him the glory of my life.

Not merely surviving anymore

but thriving and working in excellence.

After I gave the money for the book, I had a sinking feeling about this other business. I never had a partnership before and tried to do one with someone. I ended up telling them I published with another publisher and the arguments began.

On top of that, my car's transmission went out. I had to get a rental car. I was going to an interview for a coding program with Guiding Currents. I thought it went well but after I went back to my car, I had a parking ticket. That past summer consisted of work, overtime, and parking tickets. It was like no mattered where I parked the security would get me. Each ticket was $45.00 each.

I really tried to not let these outward circumstances get to me. Earlier that year, they wanted me to go to another department and help with passports. But somehow they found out about my technical background in computers so they wanted me in Informational Technology- Business Services. I thought this would be easy as well until I found out it was a federal position and I had to have a clearance. So, they had to do a credit check on me. I couldn't have over $10,000 of credit card debt. I didn't have that much credit card debt but I still had my private school loans. I was worried about that affecting me for the position.

The clearance came back good. I just needed to get my certifications in IT. I thought to myself, they offered the classes here, so I can sign up easy. The classes had already started so I had to wait until the next year. So, the rest of that summer, I worked overtime. I stopped getting SSI because I was working full-time.

Poem typed 6/19/17

I know God's truth, walk in His light,

pursue the desires He placed in my heart

and learned to walk upright.

I faced my fears even wrote them a letter,

now I am conquering my barriers

even failures that keep me down.

  I received a letter on July 22, 2016 that I was no longer considered disabled. Was it bittersweet? Maybe... I had gotten used to the disability checks but health was more important than that. It was a letter of freedom to me. I didn't get the disability checks either unless I made less money. The next day, July 23, 2016 was the Fashion for Flint Water Crisis, a charity event with the Walk Fashion Show. This show had several designers including my cousin Marc. Most of the models came from Detroit.

8/2016

Trust God.

Things have been shaky.

My eyes playing tricks on me,

living by faith verses what I see,

not letting my eyes been tricked by the enemy.

I must trust you God,

even if I think I can't trust anyone else.

I must trust God not the bills I see, not the

bills I see, not the problems that keep chasing after me.

I know I feel like I'm walking through a dark tunnel,

running to the light at the end of the tunnel.

You're there, God with your arms wide open.

Child-like faith is what I need, I will succeed.

On a Tuesday, September 20th I received my first batch of books from the publisher. I had an author's showcase at the Royal Oak Library with three other authors. This event was with "Women Who Inspire." We had to go up and speak about our book. The lady who helped create the event gave us a couple of minutes to present.

9/23/16

Speak life

I'm looking at things with my natural eye.

How things may seem to be crumbling down,

drought everywhere around.

Sometimes most of the times I want to complain and frown,

but I'm learning to speak life, speak the word.

The enemy wants me to complain,

to get frustrated find someone to blame.

I have to admit sometimes I fall into this trap,

but I know the word works so I must speak it.

September 23, 2016 was the night of elegance for me. AWAOA is a writing group that I joined that year. It was our book launch/signing in a sense. Some were able to go up there and speak about our books. I had a table in the back. I had my friend and her husband came as well. They saw a lot of people from various churches. It was like a church reunion in a sense. Some supported me because they knew me, while others bought the book because they knew someone or were the person with the auto-immune disease.

Chapter Eight

2017

I was back to school, I was an android developer, and received IT certification at Aldan for the military. I was also learning the "business side of fashion, working with Glam Box Boutique, celebrating my 37th birthday and working on debt from last flare-up.

2/24/17

Covered, hidden in God,

protected. Safe in God's arms

in the palm of His hand,

stripping away lack, depression, heaviness,

shame, rejection, feeling misunderstood

put on my garments of praise

worshipping God, praying to God

to take the pain away.

When I feel powerless and weak,

God is my strength.

The enemy may try to take things from me

my voice, my dignity but God restores me

and gives me the victory.

Despite how I feel, always do things unto the Lord,

my life is worship.

March was my birthday month and the pray like a wife

challenge.

In April, I was given a contract to write a software

program to detect parasites in the water.

4/20/17

I already went to one of these meetings but had to go

again. I dealt with sexual harassment at my job at Aldan. At

first, I didn't really see it that way, until I started telling my

sister. This guy at my job was always talking to all the

ladies. He was a lot older than me. I befriended him, along

with another woman when I started working there back in 2015. She ended up losing her job over someone bullying her because of how slowly she sewed. She was about to fight her over it but instead she left. But I continued to be this man's friend and eat lunch with him. Everyone at my job thought we were seeing each other but it was just a friendship. I was warned from several different people to watch out for him but I thought it was harmless. He seemed like a nice person. I did start noticing how he made another one of my friends uncomfortable with his odd remarks. I just thought he was joking. Everyone where I worked was dealing with a physical or mental disability. I found out his disability was mental, from a bad car accident that messed with his memory and reading ability. So, I would blame his condition on the bad behavior I would see. This went on for about a year or so before I published my first book. This was when things turned a bit strange. I would be driving to work, and he would say he was driving right next to my car. I was thinking this was odd because I never saw him in either car while I was driving. So, I just forgot about it.

One day, I ended up eating lunch with another one of my co-workers. He approached our table and said he saw me at the store after work. I thought it was no big deal. However, the next day, he said the same thing. My other co-worker asked, "Are you following Francine?" He just put his head down and walked away. I was thinking this is what they were warning me about. So, I started doing other things before I went home. My apartment complex was not too far from the store I would go to, actually a street away. It seemed not to help because one day I was on the phone with my sister Tammy and received another call on the line. I ignored it because I really needed to talk to my sister. After talking to her, I listened to my voicemail. My friend from work was at my apartment complex outside of my apartment. He left a message saying he saw my car and was picking up ads from a bulletin he put up. He has a house washing business. I had to be "blue clues" right now. An apartment and a house are two different things. If a person lives in an apartment complex, they don't need to have their house washed. He'd followed me again. I thought about all the random things he'd said and done over the past two years: wanting me to visit him at his home, always asking for a ride home, making little remarks about being special to me and now, following me. So, I had to evaluate the friendship, I had to let it go. If I continued in a friendship like this, I think I would ended up being one of his girlfriends which I really didn't want. He was 50 and I am only in my 30's. Plus the relationship was unhealthy for me.

This year I found out it was harassment. I ended up telling someone on my job a year ago. They really didn't do anything. I just kept saying he had a girlfriend. I didn't care that he had a girlfriend. I didn't want to be the "other girlfriend". He thought we were cool, but he think again. I left him alone cold turkey. I dealt with incest as a child so I am very protective of myself. I didn't know if this guy liked me sexually or not but there was a clear line between work and home. I also remembered when I was getting my muscle back because I was exercising with my cousin who was a personal trainer. He started giving me compliments on my body, but I didn't mind those. I just don't like people following me home.

4/2017

The strength of a woman - strong enough for a man but PH balanced for a woman.

I thought my strength was in my performance, what car I drove, how many figures were in my bank account and having props and shout outs.

I was quickly reminded that my strength as a woman was my personality, kindness, and caring, having healthy relationships, being healthy, not showing off everything I owned but being compassionate, humble and having self-control.

My strength was in being a help-mate, pure, effective and

modest, leaning on the grace of God, and I was thankful to

see another day.

It was good to have a good performance, to have a good car

to drive, to be able to give more, but strength comes from

God, the joy of the Lord is my strength.

To have a quiet and meek spirit, to learn to love

unconditional, to be a blessing.

Forward

Don't look over your shoulders for too long,

there are some good memories to hold on.

Set your eyes to what lies ahead,

a new beginning has begun forward

look forward to what is ahead.

God knows my chapters of my life in the order they should go, look forward to grow, to expand to reach heights to trust His plan for your life.

He knows your desires. He knows your heart.

God knows where the pages if your life will start, begin and end.

Finding an ending to this last and final memoir. I guess I can end it the way I started it. I am supposed to go to a high school reunion cruise for the class of 1998. It would be our 20th year anniversary as graduates.

I had been taking classes for mobile apps at Inkster Rack night this past February 2017. I also signed up for Huron Rack. For some reason, I wanted to solve this problem or at least help. I went to form a group of three for the quarterly finals. We got out in the first round and I was selling books in another part of Detroit and had a photoshoot the same day. I ended up getting a parking ticket by Tech Town.

They said I parked by a bus stop. On top of that the day before, I went to a high school for health and wellness day to talk about what I went through with lupus. When I went to my car, my axle broke. I had to get the tow truck to take my car to Detroit axle. The driver said, "Dave will take care of you." He was reasonable in price. I really was saving my money to double to pay a bill to match at work. Paying for this new axle messed me up. I had to look on the bright side, at least I had something to drive.

With all of this going on, my job was finally allowing me to take IT classes though the job. It started in August of this year. I also received a bid to vendor in April 2017 for cleaning the parasites out of the water. I prayed that we actually get it.

I found out in July 2017 that we didn't get the vendor. Maybe I was overwhelmed by it. It was the biggest contract to lose though. I was really disappointed. Almost every person we handed the contract to, left the project itself. The company claimed they lost our contract. I left it alone after that. My other businesses was starting to pick up. I just thought maybe God didn't want us to do the project or I didn't pray enough for it. After all, they are still fixing the Flint Water Crisis problem.

There was an article in The New York Times about the Flint Water Crisis. Most of the causes of death linked backed to the water problem. They discovered there was a disease linked to the water crisis. Several outbreaks, rashes, diseases took place. A few people died and/or were hospitalized because of the water.

Genesis 50:20
As for you, you meant evil against me, but God meant it for good in order to bring about this present outcome, that many people would be kept alive [as they are this day].

Genesis 41:38-42
Then Pharaoh said to Joseph, "Since [your] God has shown you all this, there is no one as discerning and clear-headed and wise as you are. 40 You shall have charge over my house, and all my people shall [c]be governed according to your word and pay respect [to you with reverence, submission, and obedience]; only in [matters of] the throne will I be greater than you [in Egypt]." 41 Then

Pharaoh said to Joseph, "See, I have set you [in charge]
over all the land of Egypt." 42 Then Pharaoh took off his
signet ring from his hand and put it on Joseph's hand, and
dressed him in [official] vestments of fine linen and put a
gold chain around his neck.

In August, I started my transition/change. It was something I was aiming for years, getting into the IT field. I had been taking Girl Developer classes, Sisters code, everything I could think of with code or program in it. But finally my job was allowing me to take AT certification at work. I would lose eight hours of work a week so I really had to figure out ways to make extra money. If I passed, I would be at a different building working at Flagon under business services, in federal government building. I started the classes next week. I also found out more IT certifications once I am over there. They paid better plus health insurance is covered and federal holidays.

Also for years, I just knew myself as the woman with the issue of blood. This was not my identity. I am a part of a group on Facebook called "Proverb 31 Woman." I never tried to identify with this woman in the scripture. I actually ran from her. She seemed perfect, multi-functional or something. So, I may be experiencing an issue of blood. However I am a Proverbs 31 woman even though I don't have my husband and children yet. The scripture said, "He that findeth a wife, find a good thing." I am focused on being a wife now.

Proverbs 31 10-31 amplified

[d]An excellent woman [one who is spiritual, capable, intelligent, and virtuous], who is he who can find her? Her value is more precious than jewels and her worth is far above rubies or pearls.

11 The heart of her husband trusts in her [with secure confidence],And he will have no lack of gain.

12 She comforts, encourages, and does him only good and not evil All the days of her life.

13 She looks for wool and flax And works with willing hands in delight.

14 She is like the merchant ships [abounding with

treasure];She brings her [household's] food from far away.

15 She rises also while it is still night

And gives food to her household

And assigns tasks to her maids.

16 She considers a field before she buys or accepts it

[expanding her business prudently];

With her profits she plants fruitful vines in her vineyard.

17 She equips herself with strength [spiritual, mental, and

physical fitness for her God-given task]

And makes her arms strong.

18 She sees that her gain is good;

Her lamp does not go out, but it burns continually through

the night [she is prepared for whatever lies ahead].

19 She stretches out her hands to the [e]distaff,

And her hands hold the spindle [as she spins wool into

thread for clothing].

20 She opens and extends her hand to the poor,

And she reaches out her filled hands to the needy.

21 She does not fear the snow for her household,

For all in her household are clothed in [expensive] scarlet [wool].

22 She makes for herself coverlets, cushions, and rugs of tapestry. Her clothing is linen, pure and fine, and purple [wool].

23 Her husband is known in the [city's] gates,

When he sits among the elders of the land.

24 She makes [fine] linen garments and sells them;

And supplies sashes to the merchants.

25 Strength and dignity are her clothing and her position is strong and secure; And she smiles at the future [knowing that she and her family are prepared].

26 She opens her mouth in [skillful and godly] wisdom,

And the teaching of kindness is on her tongue [giving counsel and instruction].

27 She looks well to how things go in her household,

And does not eat the bread of idleness.

28 Her children rise up and call her blessed (happy,

prosperous, to be admired);

Her husband also, and he praises her, saying,

29 "Many daughters have done nobly, and well [with the

strength of character that is steadfast in goodness],

[f]But you excel them all."

30 Charm and grace are deceptive, and [superficial]

beauty is vain, but a woman who fears the Lord [reverently

worshiping, obeying, serving, and trusting Him with awe-

filled respect], she shall be praised.

31 Give her of the product of her hands,

And let her own works praise her in the gates [of the city].

Say this prayer out loud right now:

"Dear God, I want to be a part of your family. You said in

Your Word that if I acknowledge that You raised Jesus from

the dead, and that I accept Him as my Lord and Savior, I

would be saved. So, God, I now say that I believe You

110

raised Jesus from the dead and that He is alive and well. I

accept Him now as my personal Lord and Savior. I accept

my salvation from sin right now.

I am now saved. Jesus is my Lord. Jesus is my Savior.

Thank you, Father God, for forgiving me, saving me, and

giving me eternal life with You. Amen!"

35620767R00063

Made in the USA
Columbia, SC
21 November 2018